Surveys

Contents

Teachers' notes

Aim of this book

The aim of this book is to provide you with well-presented and mathematically valuable supplementary material which will link with your existing scheme of work for mathematics, and which children will also enjoy using. To help you make the best use of the activities, please read the notes which follow.

Printing

Although photocopying on to white paper may be the simplest way for you to copy the activities in this book, do consider other alternatives. Some pages benefit from copying directly on to card, while others look much more interesting when printed on coloured paper or card. If your school does not have the facilities to do this, you may be able to have copies made using a duplicator or printing machine at a larger primary school or secondary school close to you, or perhaps at a teachers' centre.

To keep re-usable cards or worksheets in good condition, put them inside plastic wallets, laminate them, or cover them with clear sticky plastic. Even copies made on paper are surprisingly strong when covered.

Record-keeping and storage

We have not provided a separate system of record-keeping for these activities, as most teachers prefer to add to their existing scheme of records. You could use the child's own maths writing book to make a note of activities used, when this would be helpful information to have.

Worksheets can usually be fastened into the child's book using a piece of sticky tape at the side, like an extra page in the book, as an obvious reminder of an activity completed.

Mathematical content

This book is about collecting and handling data. The children are encouraged to survey their peers, and to record data they have collected in different ways. They are introduced to tallies, frequency tables and graphs. They are encouraged to discuss, interpret and compare their surveys. Many of the activities are open-ended and allow children to work at their own levels. The same starting point may result in different graphical representations depending on each child's previous experience.

Every activity needs introducing by the teacher if the children are to make the most of it. Sometimes, activities may be taken home to share with parents and other family members.

Notes on individual activities

Page 5: Babies

Some children may wish to record the number of babies by placing a number next to each group, while others may wish to remember the number of babies each animal has. The children can also write the name or draw a picture of the animal with the most babies. Others may identify the correct animals by colouring only them in.

Page 6: Friends

The children could go on from this survey to do the survey card on 'Playground games'. It is important not to make the children feel upset if they have played by themselves at playtime.

Page 7: Weather

This weather survey is related to a specific time, that is coming to school, so that the children are not confused by several different types of weather during the day. Even if it rains they may not record this as a day when they got wet as they may have come to school in a car.

Pages 8 and 9: Holidays and Holiday homes

All the pictures of different holiday destinations or holiday homes may be coloured in at the beginning or the children may be asked to colour in just the most popular holiday destination or home. The children have to record their friends' choices for their holiday in the box below each picture.
This could be as a tick or the children could be introduced to a tally.

You may wish the children to record the total number of children they have asked and compare their results with other children.

Some children may be able to develop their own surveys about holidays.

Pages 10 and 11: Choose a T-shirt and Choose a badge

The children may record their friends' choices by placing a tick next to the preferred T-shirt or badge or by using a tally. If the children wish to ask their friends to choose between more than four they will need extra copies of these sheets.

Page 12: Choose your pets

Having drawn themselves in the circle and an extra animal in the spare square, the children have to tick the animals they would choose as pets. The children could also indicate their choices by drawing arrows from the self-portrait to the favourite pet or by colouring in only the animals they would like to keep as pets, rather than all the animals.

Page 13: Pets

There is one spare space for the children to draw another animal to include in this survey. All the pictures of pets may be coloured in at the beginning or the children could be asked to colour in just the most popular pet. The children have to record their friends' choices of a pet in the box below each picture. This could be as a tick or they could be introduced to a tally. You may wish the children to record the total number of people questioned or to compare their results with others and/or to record the information they have collected in the form of a graph.

Page 14: Pets or not?

There are spaces for at least six children to be asked whether or not they have a pet at home. It is important that children who do not have pets are not made to feel uncomfortable. The child undertaking the survey could write down each child's name or could ask the children to write their own names on the lines. The child doing the survey then has to total up the number of children's names in each list. This information could then be recorded as a graph. Interesting discussions can occur when different children are asked to compare their results.

Page 15: Cubes

Interlocking cubes may be used, but the cubes must all be the same size. You may wish the children to make rules for this survey, such as the cubes must not be interlocked or that the children have to be able to turn their hands over without dropping any of the cubes. This activity could be followed up by the children surveying other people. These results could be recorded on extra copies of this sheet which have the instruction in the top box changed to 'Draw a friend' and the instruction in the bottom box changed to 'Draw another friend'. The results of the whole class could be collected and the children may begin to develop their own ways of recording these results.

Pages 16 and 17: Transport and Transport survey

The children could use the transport pictures to devise their own survey sheet or they can be used for the 'Transport survey' page. The pictures should be coloured in, cut out and stuck on to the survey sheet to record how the children have travelled. The children can use this sheet in two different ways. They can just fill it in as a graph with numbers along the bottom or they can put the names of the children they ask along the bottom and record each child's answers in a column as in a Carroll diagram.

The children could go on to use the survey card 'More about transport'.

Pages 18 and 19: Storytime – 1 and Storytime – 2

The children can survey their friends to find out which of these two stories they would like you to read at storytime. The children can copy the title of the most popular story at the bottom of the page or be asked just to colour in the most popular book. Children's names could be written on the lines next to the pictures or, if a lot of children are to be questioned, the children's preferences could be indicated by ticks or a tally. They should then move on to do their own survey using 'Storytime – 2'.

'Storytime – 2' enables children to select and draw their own books in the spaces. If the choice is between more than two stories they will need to be given additional copies of this sheet.

Pages 20 and 21: Coming to school – 1 and Coming to school – 2

The children can draw pictures of the people they question in the appropriate sections of this Venn diagram. Alternatively, they could write the children's names in the correct section or ask them to write their own names on the sheet. The information can be interpreted on 'Coming to school – 2'. Some children may already have asked their friends how they came to school if they did not come by car. If they have not found out this information they will have to look at their first survey sheet and question again the children who did not come by car.

Pages 22 and 23: Fruit – 1 and Fruit – 2

The graphs should be coloured in first and then the children should use the graphs to find out how many children selected each fruit and which were the most and least popular fruits.

Pages 24 and 25: Games and Games graph

The survey has already been carried out on the 'Games' sheet but the children have to add up the number of children who can play each game. They may need to be shown how a tally can be counted in fives. The information from this frequency table can then be recorded as a graph on the 'Games graph'. The children may be able to survey the games children in their own class can play if this sheet is copied with the tallies obliterated by pieces of plain paper. Others may wish to devise their own data collection sheets with their own choices of games.

The 'Games graph' can be used to record the information from the 'Games' page or to record information from the children's own games surveys. Some children may be able to write down questions about their completed graphs for others to answer.

Page 26: Fastenings

On this page the children have to record information about how their friends' shoes fasten.

They may wish to record the information first on a separate piece of paper so that they do not make any mistakes on the graph. You may wish to ask the children how they are going to ensure that they do not ask the same people twice. They could also be asked to record the numbers of children they have questioned. There is one spare space in case the children have shoes that fasten in another way. It is interesting for the children to compare their graphs with those of others.

Pages 27–32: A5 survey cards

The last six pages in this book each provide you with two separate A5 survey cards. The children should consider what information they need to collect, how they are going to collect it and how they are going to record the information. It is a good idea for the children to try out their questions and survey sheets on a small sample of children, perhaps four, and then make any alterations that are needed before they use them to collect the information needed for their survey. If the children draw pictures on their survey sheets, it will usually help them to remember the choices they are offering or the questions they are asking.

More about fruit and More about transport

You may first wish the children to complete 'Fruit – 1' and 'Fruit – 2' before completing their own fruit survey. The children could do further fruit surveys by finding out which was the last fruit their friends ate, which fruits they dislike or which fruit they have in their packed lunches.

Before making their own transport survey you may wish children to complete the previous 'Transport survey' page. Some children may wish to do further transport surveys by finding out how their friends get to the shops, the models or colours of their friends' families' cars, what forms of transport their friends travelled on last time they went on holiday or which form of transport they would like to go on.

Television survey and Songs survey

The children could develop other television surveys. They could try to find out what television programmes their friends watched last night or what their parents like to watch. The children may need a television guide to help them with the names of the programmes.

The children may survey songs they sing themselves or pop songs or both. They may need some songbooks to help them with the song titles.

Story survey and Sandwich survey

You may wish the children to have completed 'Storytime – 1' and 'Storytime – 2' before they begin this story survey. This could be a survey of which stories the children like to read or which stories they like to hear. They could go on to do a survey of which stories their parents like to tell.

The sandwich survey can be interpreted as which sort of bread or which sort of filling the children like in their sandwiches. They could do further surveys about their friends' packed lunches.

Going home and Drinks survey

If the children go home with a variety of different people or are not quite sure who is going to collect them from school, you may wish to specify that the survey is about whom they went home with yesterday. A similar survey could be taken of who brings the children to school.

The drinks survey could be followed by the children doing a survey to find out who likes milk, or what people had to drink before they came to school or what drink people have in their packed lunches.

The happy survey and Playground games

Having completed 'The happy survey', the children could, perhaps, do a survey about what makes them cross.

You may wish the children to complete the 'Friends' survey before they go on to do a survey of playground games. They could do surveys of the most popular games or who taught them the games.

Magic wishes and Home from school

Having completed the 'Magic wishes' survey, the children may like to think of three things they would wish for and ask their friends to place them in order of preference.

The children could follow on the 'Home from school' survey by finding out what was the first thing their friends did when they got home yesterday or what they would like to do when they get home tonight.

National Curriculum: Mathematics

In addition to the content of AT1, up to and including Level 3, the following statements of attainment from AT5 are relevant to the activities in this book:

Level 1
(a) Sort a set of objects, describing the criteria chosen.
Level 2
(a) Interpret relevant data which have been collected.
Level 3
(a) Access information in a simple database.
(b) Construct and interpret statistical diagrams.

Scottish 5–14 Curriculum: Mathematics

In addition to the content of the attainment outcome 'Problem solving and enquiry', the following attainment outcome and targets are relevant to the activities in this book:

Attainment outcome	Strand	Attainment targets	Level
Information handling	Collect	By obtaining information for a task from a picture or story; By collecting information about themselves and familiar objects.	A
		By obtaining information for a task from sets of pictures or diagrams; By conducting a class survey.	B
	Organise	By tallying as collections of objects; By counting; By sorting into specific sets (shape, colour, texture).	A
		By a tallying sheet with individual ticks for each item; By using a simple database in which the teacher defines the headings or fields.	B
	Display	By using real objects; By using pictures; By obtaining simple diagrams such as one-to-one mappings.	A
		By using tables, charts or diagrams, such as mapping one to many; By constructing a bar graph with axes graduated in units and with discrete categories of information.	B
	Interpret	From displays by locating and counting.	A
		From displays by asking specific questions including some about similarities and differences.	B

◆ **Name** ______________________

Babies

◆ Who has the most babies? ______________________

◆ Name ____________________

Friends

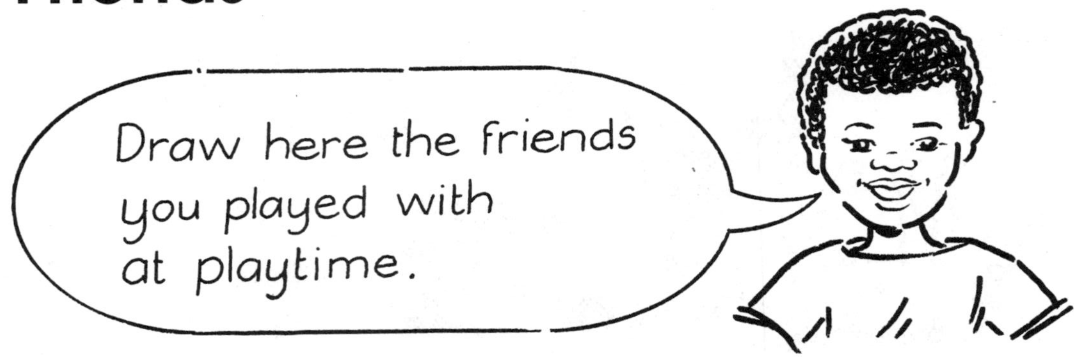

◆ How many people did you play with? ____________________

◆ **Name** ______________________

Weather

Monday

Tuesday

Wednesday

Thursday

Friday

◆ On which days did you get wet? ______________________

◆ Name ______________________

Holidays

◆ Ask your friends which one of these places they would like to go to for their holidays.

◆ Use the boxes to show which place they choose.

◆ Name ______________________

Holiday homes

◆ Ask your friends which one of these homes they would like to live in on holiday.

◆ Use the boxes to show which home they choose.

◆ **Name** ______________________

Choose a T-shirt

- Draw 4 T-shirt designs.
- Ask your friends which T-shirt they like the most.

◆ **Name** ______________________________

Choose a badge

- Draw 4 badge designs.
- Ask your friends which badge they like the most.

◆ Name ______________________

Choose your pets

- Draw yourself in the circle.
- Draw an extra animal in the square.
- Tick the animals you would choose as pets.

◆ Name ______________________

Pets

◆ Ask your friends which animals they would like to have as pets.

◆ Use the boxes to show which pets they choose.

◆ Name ______________________

Pets or not?

These children have pets.

These children do not have pets.

____

____

____

____

____

____

____

____

____

____

☐ children have pets.

☐ children do not have pets.

◆ Name ____________________

Cubes

◆ How many cubes can you hold in one hand?
◆ Colour in one square for each cube.

◆ Draw yourself.

◆ Draw a friend.

◆ Name ______________________

Transport

◆ Colour in and cut out these pictures to use in your transport survey.

◆ Name ____________________

Transport survey

◆ Ask 5 friends whether they have been in a car, an aeroplane or a bus. Use the pictures on the transport page to stick on here and record your results.

◆ Name ______________________________

Storytime – 1

◆ Find out which of these 2 stories people would like at storytime.

____

____

____

____

____

____

◆ Which story did most people choose?

◆ Name ____________________

Storytime – 2

◆ Find out which of these stories people would like at storytime.

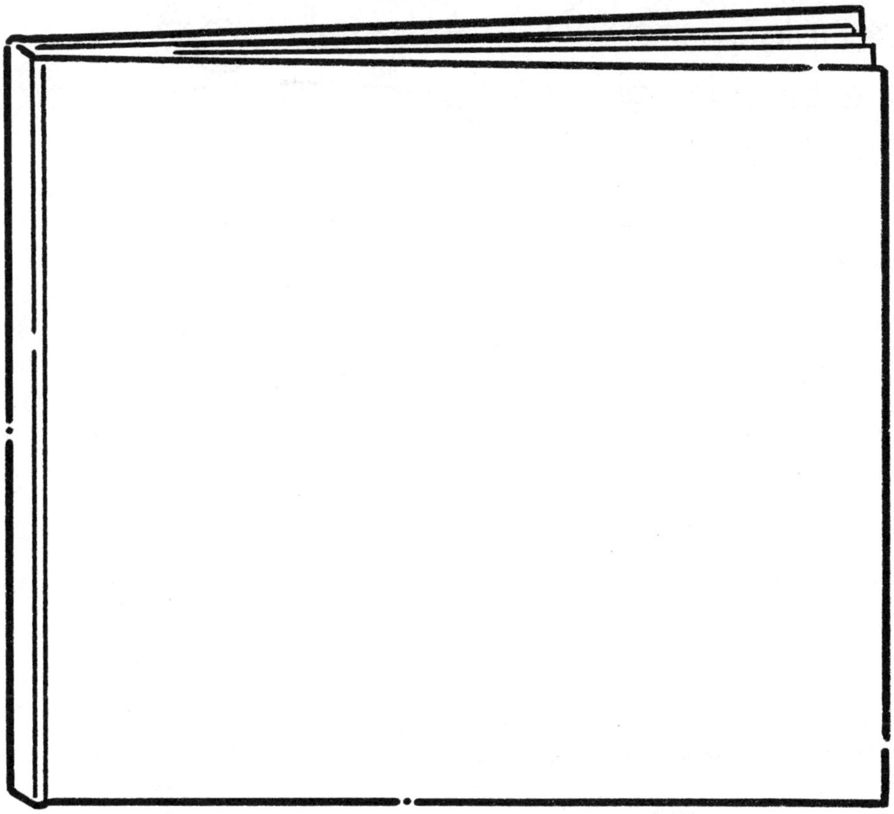

____

____

____

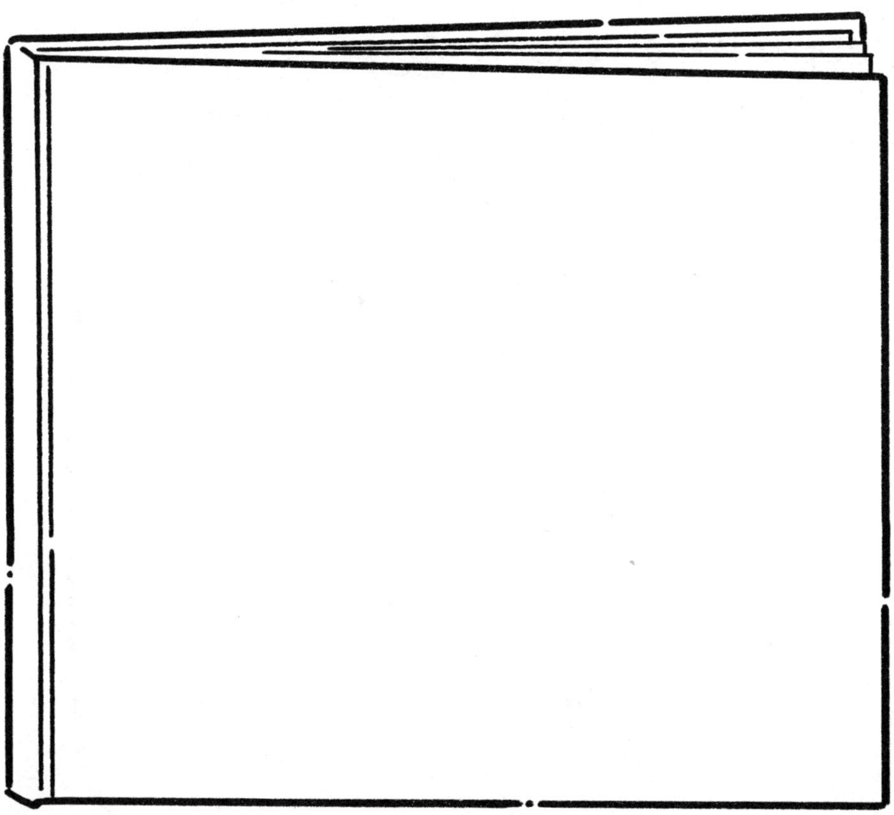

____

____

____

◆ Which story did most people choose?

◆ **Name** ______________________

Coming to school – 1

◆ Name ______________________

Coming to school – 2

I asked ☐ people how they came to school.

☐ people came to school by car.

☐ people did not come to school by car.

◆ **Name** ______________________

Fruit – 1

◆ How many children liked each fruit?

◆ Name ______________________________

Fruit – 2

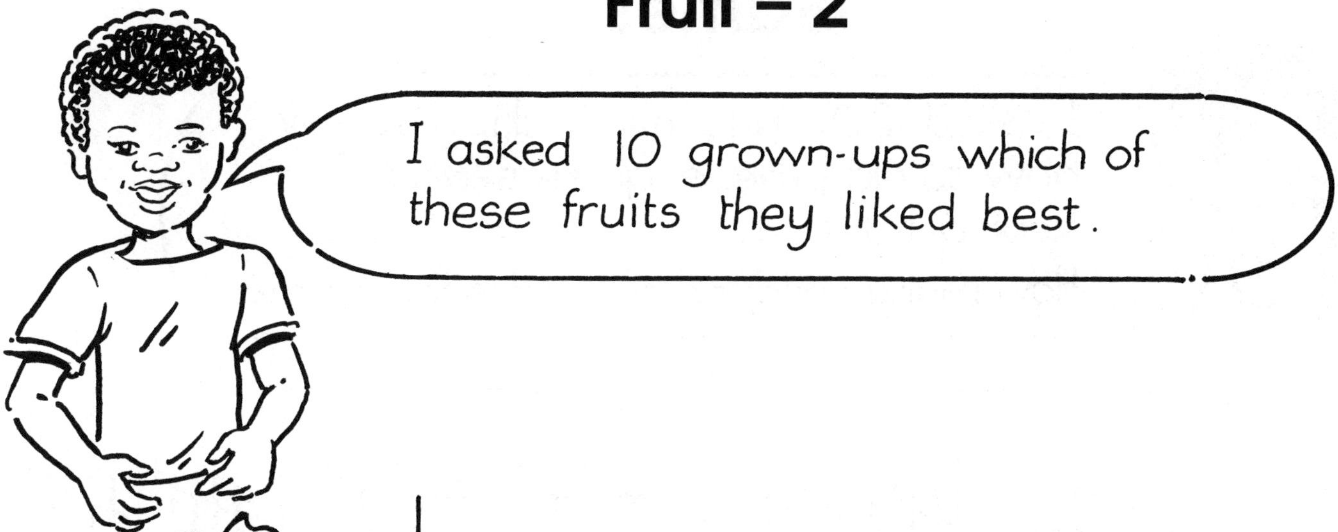

◆ Draw the most popular fruit here.

◆ Draw the least popular fruit here.

◆ **Name** ______________________

Games

I asked 20 children if they knew how to play these games and I kept a tally.
How many children played each game ?

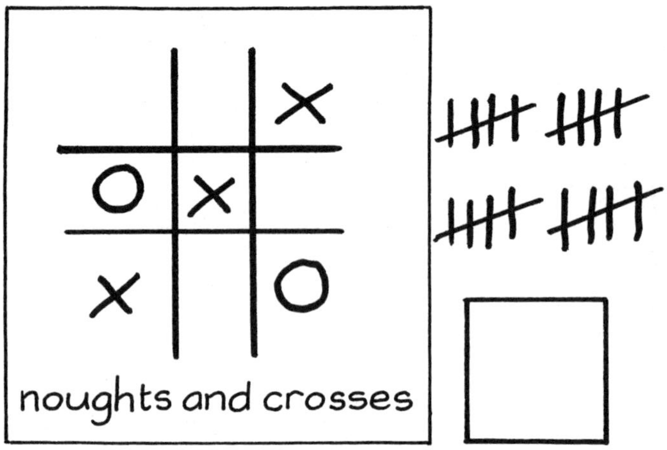

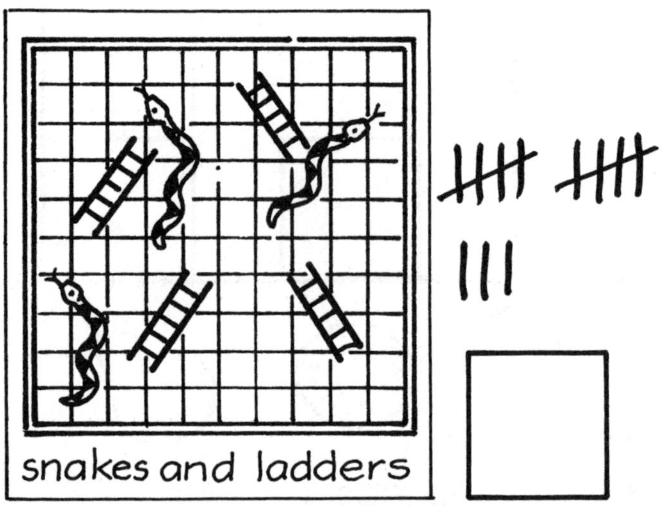

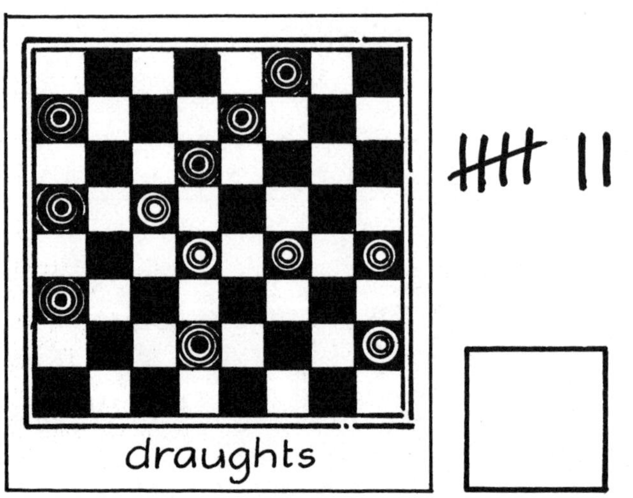

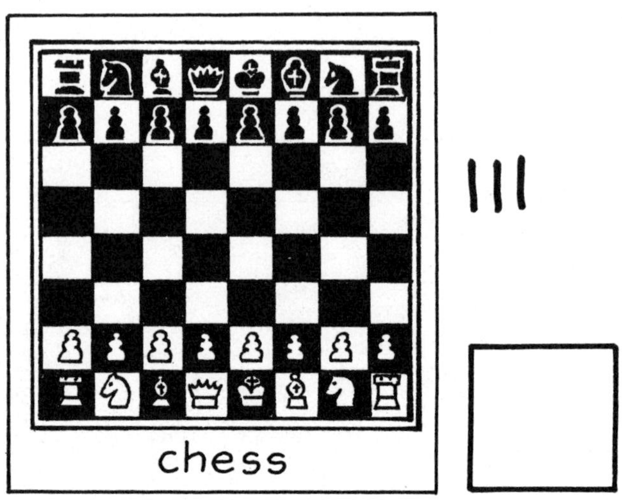

◆ **Name** ______________________

Games graph

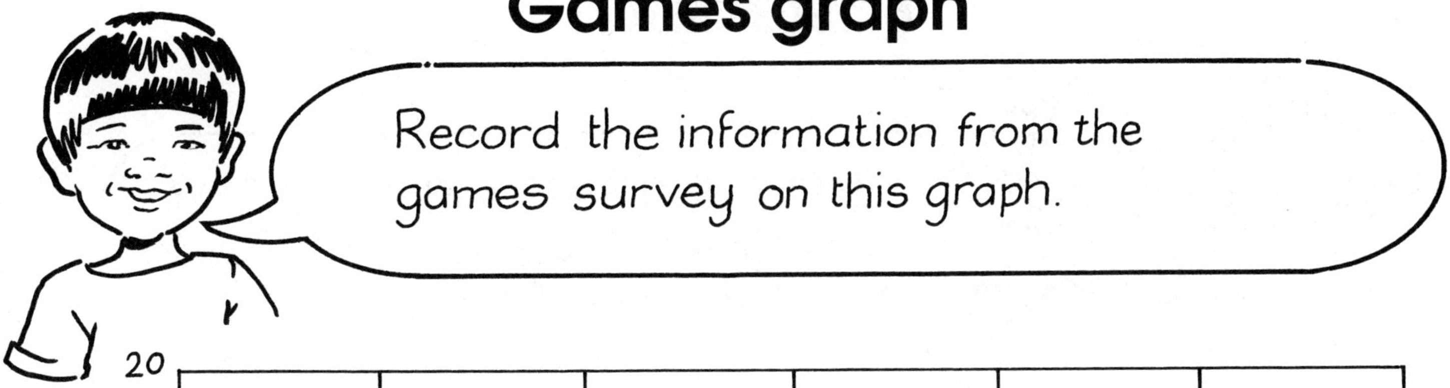

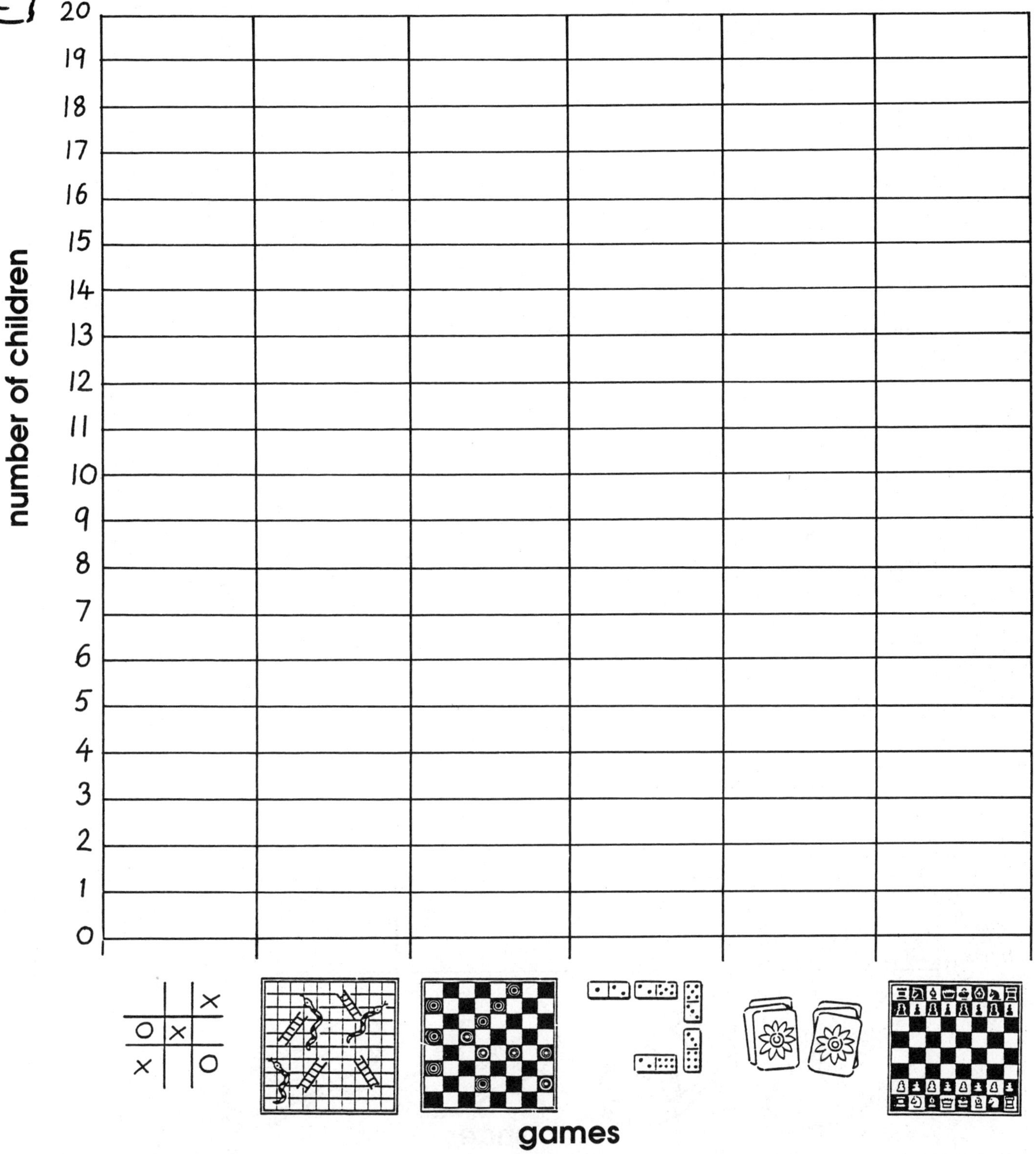

◆ **Name** ______________________

Fastenings

Colour in a rectangle to show how your shoes fasten.
Now ask your friends.

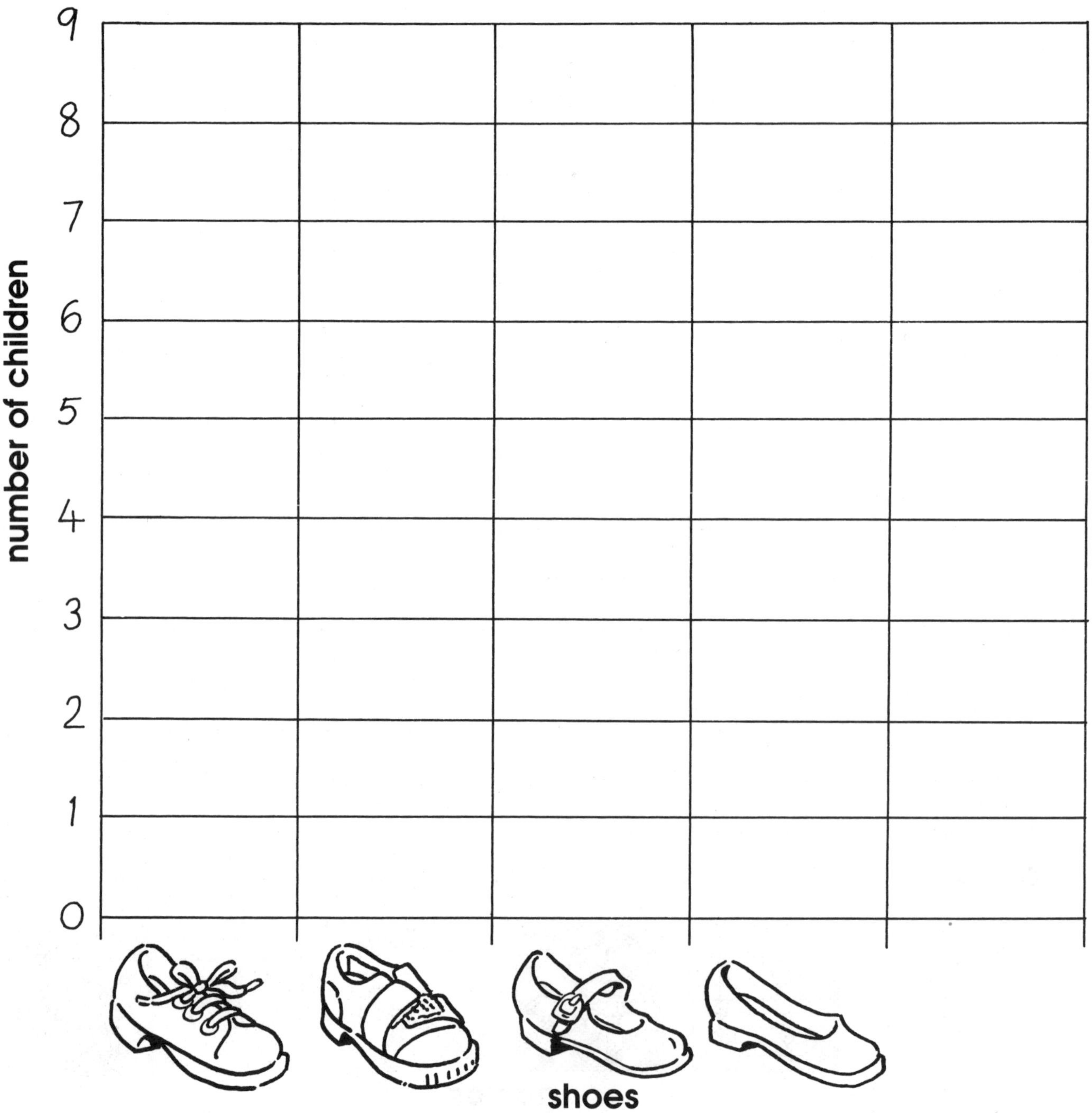

More about fruit

More about transport

Television survey

Songs survey

Story survey

Sandwich survey

Going home

Drinks survey

The happy survey

Playground games

Magic wishes

Home from school